# THE COURAGE TO SAY "F*** IT!"



ANDRE ELCHAM

Disclaimer: The author has used generative AI in writing up to 15% of the content of this publication.

Self-published by Andre Elcham 2026.



Contact to request copies of this book or permission to reproduce or use quotes or images from any part of this book:

andre_elcham@mac.com

ISBN: 978-0-646-73599-3

1. Self-help techniques

2. Business

This self-published book has been produced by:

*On Time Typing Books and Life Stories*

www.ontimetyping.com ; info@ontimetyping.com

- Editors: Kyla-Jayne Rajah and Sally-Anne Watson Kane
- Design: Claire McGregor

# Contents

**YOU JUST NEED ONE DECISION BRAVE ENOUGH TO CHANGE YOUR DIRECTION.**

# Introduction

Every day, whether you realise it or not, you're making decisions that shape your path. Some decisions feel minor - what coffee to order, whether to hit snooze, what email to ignore until tomorrow.

Other decisions come with a little more weight - career changes, investments, relationships, strategy. The big stuff. The stuff that keeps you up at night pretending to scroll your phone, while quietly your mind is spiralling.

Let's be honest, decision making isn't always a graceful process. Most of the time, it's full of second guessing, thinking about worst-case scenarios, asking 12 people for their opinion and still ending up exactly where you started: stuck.

We all know the feeling of circling the same idea over and over, caught between "what if I regret this?" and "what if I don't do anything and still regret that too?"

The 50/50 zone is the most unproductive place; I know it well, I've been there many times. That's exactly why I wrote this book.

I believe decision making is something you can get better at. It's not reserved for CEOs or those annoyingly decisive people, who always seem to have a five-year plan (and a backup five-year plan).

*No, it's simpler than that. Most of the time, all you need is a little courage, some belief, and a decision to act.*

This book is straightforward and keeps it real. It blends a few things: real-life stories, hard truths, some humour (because we need it), and plenty of practical takeaways—no fluff, just tools, frameworks, and perspectives that work in the real world, whether you're leading a company, running a side hustle, switching careers, or trying to decide whether to send that risky text.

I'll also let you in on the simple mantra that I use whenever I feel stuck in the mud of overthinking. It's helped me push through moments of fear, perfectionism, and paralysis; and spoiler alert, it's not something you'll learn in a degree or find in your average self-help book.

It's the intelligent use of two words: "F*** It!"

Because sometimes, when you've weighed the pros and cons to death, when the timing will never be perfect, when clarity won't come until after the leap … *"F*** It"* sets everything in motion.

It's not reckless. It's release. It's the moment you've been waiting for.

So, if you've ever sat on a decision too long, chased your tail trying to find the right answer, or beat yourself up for being stuck, this book is for you.

If you're allergic to swear words, uncomfortable with honesty, or trying to win procrastinator of the year, I recommend you back away from this book, it might not be for you.

For the rest of us? It's about to get real. Let's GO!

# Chapter 1

## The 50/50 Dilemma

**WHEN IT'S 50/50, SAY "F*** IT"
AND PICK ONE—
MOVEMENT BEATS MAYBE.**

## When "F*** It" is the Most Professional Answer You'll Ever Give Yourself

Let's paint the picture. You're sitting at your desk, two options staring you in the face. You've made a pro/con list. You've overthought it. You've asked three colleagues, your spouse, and your dog. Still: nothing. You're at a 50/50.

Welcome to decision purgatory.

This is where most people stall. Not because the choices are impossible, but because they're trying to avoid regret. You want the *perfect* decision.

Newsflash: Perfect is a fantasy people chase when they're too scared to move.

## The Case for "F*** It"

Enter the "F*** It" principle.

It's not reckless. It's decisive. It's the mental release valve that lets you stop circling and *move*. It's your way of giving yourself permission to act when logic and emotion are in deadlock.

Let's go through a few real-life (and totally relatable) examples.

## *Scenario 1*

### Real-World "F*** It" Moment of Starting my First Business and Launching Vespa Fashion.

Years ago, I was working full-time, doing the 9-to-5 (plus some unpaid overtime, of course), and I had this itch. A *business idea*, specifically, in retail and wholesale fashion.

On paper, I had absolutely no reason to pursue it. I didn't have a design degree. I wasn't connected to Milan or Paris. I didn't even know how wholesale buying worked at the time. But I *did* have this fire to create something of my own.

I spent weeks going back and forth. One day I'd say, "This could actually work!" The next day I'd say, "This is dumb, stick to your lane." I repeated that cycle for about six months.

Eventually, after one too many PowerPoints and the pressing realisation that I was building someone else's dream, I looked in the mirror and said: "F*** it!!! I'm opening a fashion store."

And I did. *Vespa Fashion* was born.

Was I ready? Not really. Did I have all the answers? Nope. But I figured it out. I sourced products, negotiated with suppliers, did the marketing myself (and it showed, my first logo looked like it was made in WordArt), and I opened the doors.

The first customer walked in, looked around, and said, "Is this a scooter shop?"

(Not the brand identity I was going for, and I did have a Vespa scooter on display in the front window, but hey, foot traffic is foot traffic.)

The business grew. I learned. I adapted. I even started understanding what customers wanted, beyond just "something black in a size medium."

It was chaotic, rewarding, and humbling. But without that "F*** It" moment, it never would've happened. Vespa would've stayed in my head, not on the shopfront. The logo would still be scribbled in a notebook. The ideas would still be "maybes."

That moment. The one where I stopped trying to get everything perfect and just moved was the line between dreaming and doing.

It wasn't a clean leap. It was messy. It was uncertain. But it was real. And real beats perfect every time. My "F*** It" moment gave me the green light I'd been waiting for. I gave it to myself.

## *Scenario 2:*

### Years Later. A Different Kind of Business: HR Ambassador and Launching HR Ambassador.

After I finished my journey in the fashion business, I pivoted. Not just into a new industry but a whole new way of thinking.

Human Resources had always been in my skill set. People, culture, recruitment, leadership, this was where I was strong.

I'd spent years inside companies seeing what worked (and more often, what didn't), and I knew I could do it.

Then, an idea came to start a proper HR consulting and recruitment business. Brand it. Structure it. Build a real practice.

Even with years of experience behind me, the self-doubt crept in again:

- *"What if no one takes me seriously?"*
- *"What if this becomes just another side gig?"*
- *"What if I leave a steady income and end up living off two-minute noodles and regret?"*

Classic 50/50. All the signs pointed to "go for it," but my brain kept yelling, "wait a bit longer."

Until, once again, I pulled the trigger: "F*** It! I've got this." *HR Ambassador* was born, and guess what? The market *did* take it seriously.

I landed global clients. Built partnerships. Created scalable services. Hired people. Got into boardrooms. Helped real businesses fix messy people problems. But none of that happened because I had everything perfectly planned. It happened because I *moved.*

The business didn't grow out of certainty. It grew out of momentum. I just had to give it that first kick, which, for me, sounded a lot like, "F*** It."

Ok, that's a little about my businesses and how I arrived at my "F*** It" moments. What I realised after overthinking every move, playing it safe, and trying to tick every damn box, was that none of it really moved the needle.

The second I stopped asking for permission, stopped waiting for the "right time," and just started, things began happening. Fast. Not always perfect. Not always pretty. But real progress.

It cut through the noise, the fear, the opinions, and got me to act. Action **is what** changed everything.

## It's Your Turn to Say, "F*** It"

*Scenario 3:*

### The Job Offer You're Contemplating

You're in a decent role, but you've been offered a new one. Same money, different headaches. You've been mulling it for days.

**Pros:** new title, new industry.

**Cons:** risk, change, starting over.

You're stuck.

Then one morning, over a cold coffee and a passive-aggressive email from your current boss, it hits you: "I'm going."

Not in a dramatic Jerry Maguire movie scene kind of

way, no storming out or slamming laptops shut. Just a quiet, undeniable clarity.

You're done explaining yourself. Done waiting for things to get better. Done trading your time, energy, and sanity for a paycheck that doesn't even cover the cost of who you're becoming.

It's not rage. It's freedom. And once you feel that, once *"F*** It"** lands, there's no going back.

Yes, it's uncomfortable, but within six months you're challenged, learning, and most importantly no longer stuck.

## *Scenario 4:*

### The Pitch That Wasn't Ready (But You Did It Anyway)

You've been invited to pitch to a potential client. The presentation is at 70%. You want two more days to polish it. But the meeting is *today*.

Do you cancel? Postpone? Or...

"F*** It. Speak from the heart."

You show up. Not with a flawless pitch, but with clarity, honesty, and determination. You're not perfect—but you're real. And in a world full of filters, and overproduced slideshows, *real* stands out.

You speak like a human, not a LinkedIn post. You own what you know, admit what you don't, and bring energy that can't be faked. And that lands.

They like you, because while everyone else is still rehearsing their script, you've already walked in with the truth.

*Scenario 5:*

### The Conversation You've Been Avoiding

You know you need to give feedback to a team member, but you've been avoiding it. You've rewritten the message three times. You've role-played the chat in your head. Still no action.

Until, finally, you say: **"F*** It",** I'll just be honest."

No more rehearsed lines. No more dancing around the truth to keep the peace or protect someone else's comfort.

Just clear, direct words delivered with calm conviction. You book the meeting. You speak plainly. You say what needs to be said, not to provoke, but to move.

And the outcome? Not a blow-up. Not a breakdown. Just **clarity**.

You're met with a nod, maybe even a little surprise, but also respect.

## The Hidden Professionalism in "F*** It"

Here's the twist no one tells you: "F*** It" isn't lazy. It's *efficient*. It's what happens when overthinking costs more than acting. It's the line between being frozen and being effective.

The real danger isn't in making the wrong choice. It's in making *no* choice and letting indecision eat your progress alive.

Next time you're at 50/50 and can't decide?

Say, "F*** It. I'm moving forward." And mean it.

That moment of courage might just be the most productive thing you ever do.

## The "F*** It" Framework— 3 Simple Checks

For those of you who like structure, here's a short framework to use when you're 50/50 and stuck:

### *1. Clarity*

Have you done the basics? Do you understand the risks, the options, and have you considered the pros and cons?

If yes, you're not ignorant. You're just indecisive.

### *2. Consequences*

Is this decision life-threatening or business-ending?

If no, you're dealing with a manageable risk. One you can probably recover from.

### *3. Capacity*

If it goes wrong, can you handle it? Will you learn something useful either way?

If yes, you're ready.

## Final Word

People think "F*** It" is a throwaway phrase. But used correctly, it's one of the most powerful tools in decision making. It cuts through noise. It forces clarity, and it gets you *unstuck*.

If you're sitting on the fence and you've been there for too long, the only thing you're building is splinters.

Say it. Mean it. Move.

"F*** It" might just be the best and smartest thing you ever say.

# Chapter 2

## What Happens After You Say, "F*** It"

START SCARED, START UNSURE, START MESSY, BUT START. THE REAL SHIFT DOESN'T HAPPEN WHEN YOU PLAN, IT HAPPENS WHEN YOU DECIDE YOU'RE FINALLY WILLING TO BET ON YOURSELF.

## Welcome to the Chaos (and Clarity)

So, you've said it. You hit the button. Made the call. Sent the email. Registered the business name. Signed the lease. Quit the job. Raised your hand.

"F*** it, let's go."

You've crossed the line from idea to action. Now what?

Here's the part no one tells you: After the high-five moment and the initial adrenaline hit, things get **messy**.

### Stage 1: The Buzz

The first few hours, days, or even weeks feel *electric*. You're finally moving. You feel brave. Empowered. Slightly delusional but in a good way.

You post on LinkedIn. You tell your mate. You update your email signature to say "Founder." Maybe you even order some business cards you won't use. Life is good.

You're high on momentum and caffeine. You feel *unstoppable*. Enjoy this stage. You'll need it to survive the next one.

### Stage 2: The "Oh Shit" Dip

And then ... it hits.

- You realise you don't know where to start.
- You get your first unexpected cost.

- Someone questions your idea and suddenly they sound smart and you sound like you're winging it (because ... in part, you are).
- You stare at your calendar and wonder, "what next?"

This is where most people start second-guessing the decision. This is the "oh shit" dip, and it's completely normal.

Every founder, consultant, creative, and corporate escapee goes through it. The mistake people make is assuming the dip means they were wrong. It doesn't.

It just means you're between the comfort of "known" and the reward of "figured-it-out." Push through.

## Stage 3: The Dirty Work

Once the dip stops punching you in the face, you settle into reality. It's not glamorous, but it's yours.

- You stop trying to get everything perfect.
- You get resourceful.
- You make your first $1 the hard way.
- You realise how long this road *actually* is.
- You stop saying "founder" and start saying "problem-solver."

This is the stage where you build grit, not hype. And oddly enough, this is where a lot of people start to love it. Not because it's easy but because it's *theirs*.

You're learning fast. Adapting. Failing forward. It's *working*, even if it doesn't always look like it yet.

## Stage 4: Clarity Kicks In

Somewhere along the way, usually after a few wins, a few losses, and maybe a breakdown over a silly email, you realise something: You're in control now.

Not in the "nothing goes wrong" kind of way. In the "I trust myself to handle whatever comes" kind of way.

You realise you're not trying to avoid mistakes anymore; you're trying to *grow through them*. You make better decisions, faster, you stop asking for permission, and you start making moves with intention.

## A Quick Debrief: What to Expect After "F*** It"

Here's the cycle in plain English:

| Phase | Feels Like |
|---|---|
| The Buzz | "I'm a genius. This is my moment." |
| The Dip | "What have I done?" |
| The Dirty Work | "Okay, head down. Let's build." |
| Clarity | "I've got this ... even when I don't." |

You will cycle through this loop *multiple times*. With every big move, new idea, new hire, new risk and the cycle begins again.

Each time, you move through it faster and calmer with more confidence, more tools and less panic. That's growth.

## Final Thought: Don't Confuse Discomfort with a Bad Decision

Most people hit discomfort and assume they need to reverse the decision. No. Discomfort is not failure. It's a sign that you're stretching.

If you're in Stage 2 or 3 right now and in the middle of a "what the hell was I thinking?" moment, just know you're going to be okay.

You're not lost, you're not crazy, and you're not failing! You're just *building*. You're learning and being courageous.

You said "F*** It". Now, it's time to follow through. Don't go back—build forward.

# Chapter 3

## Decision Debt—What Happens When You Don't Move

**EVERY TIME YOU CHOOSE SOMETHING, YOU SHAPE SOMEONE. THAT SOMEONE IS YOU.**

## Indecision is More Expensive Than You Think

What if, you don't say "F*** it."? What if you wait? Hesitate. Sit in the 50/50 zone, hoping clarity lands in your inbox?

If so, instead of a bold (or even messy) move forward, you're now carrying something far heavier: Decision Debt.

It's real. And it's killing momentum in boardrooms, businesses, everyday life and your own bloody brain.

## What is Decision Debt?

It's the cost you pay when you delay a decision that needs to be made. It accumulates silently, like interest on a credit card you forgot to cancel. And just like financial debt, decision debt compounds:

- **The longer you wait, the heavier it gets.**
- **The more you avoid, the more it controls you.**

Let's be clear, no amount of spreadsheets or additional team meetings will fix this problem.

## The Symptoms of Decision Debt

### *You Keep "Circling Back"*

You've had the same conversation four times. Different people. Same points. No action.

### *You're Bottlenecking Everything*

Projects can't move until you say, "yes" or "no", and you keep delaying because *you're not ready yet* (you are).

### *You're Stuck in Research Mode*

You've built the world's most beautiful spreadsheet. You're on page 19 of Google. You've bookmarked 11 podcasts that you'll never listen to. Still no decision.

### *You're Mentally Exhausted*

You haven't even *done* anything. You've just *thought* about doing something, endlessly.

Sound familiar?

## The Cost of Not Choosing

When you don't make a call, here's what *actually* happens:

| **What You Think You're Avoiding** | **What You're Actually Creating** |
|---|---|
| Making a wrong move | Delaying *any* move and outcomes |
| Looking foolish | Looking like a leader who can't decide |
| Failing fast | Failing *slowly* and painfully |
| Uncertainty | Paralysis for you *and* your team |

Worst of all, you start losing trust in yourself. You begin to doubt the next call before you even make it. You begin to train your brain to associate decisions with anxiety over action.

That's decision debt, and it doesn't just slow you down, it builds resistance to your future moves.

## Real Talk from Experience

Let me be honest, I've paid my fair share of decision interest over the years. There have been times when I stayed too long in roles, waited too long to exit a client relationship, and took *forever* to hire because I was afraid of the wrong fit.

I took *even longer* to fire someone when I knew it wasn't working, and another time I delayed launching a service because the landing page wasn't "perfect". (It still wasn't perfect when I launched it but guess what? Still worked).

Every one of those moments cost me time, energy, money, and momentum. Not because I chose wrong, but because I didn't choose at all.

## How to Break the Cycle

Want to clear your decision debt?

Here's how:

## *1. Recognise it*

Are you stuck in loops? Are things dragging? That's a flag. It's often your cue to pause, look honestly at the pattern you're in, and decide what needs to change

## *2. Name the actual fear*

Most delayed decisions come down to two things:

- Fear of looking dumb
- Fear of not being in control

Newsflash: You can look smart and still be stuck. And your ability to control anything is a myth, just ask anyone who's run a business.

## *3. Set a decision deadline*

Not a deadline to "think", but a deadline to *decide*. Put it in your calendar. Give it weight, and then stick to it.

## *4. Use the "F*** It" filter*

Revisit the three questions from Chapter 1:

- ✓ Have I thought this through?
- ✓ Is the risk survivable?
- ✓ Can I handle the fallout?

If yes. "F*** It". Let's go!

# Final Word

Sitting still doesn't mean nothing is happening. It means something *is* and it's usually the slow deterioration of opportunity. It's time to stop dragging out decisions that are holding you back.

Choose. Act. Learn. Adjust.

Even the wrong decision beats none at all. Progress punishes hesitation, whereas momentum rewards motion. The pathway will make itself clear. Clarity always follows courage—not comfort.

You can't build a future from a holding pattern. Say the words and make the move.

# Chapter 4

## Gut and Grit

**YOU ALREADY HAVE THE TOOLS. YOU'RE JUST WAITING FOR SOMEONE ELSE TO VALIDATE THEM.**

## Tools You Already Have (But Don't Trust Yet)

Let's talk tools. Not software. Not frameworks. Not a 12-step process made by someone in a TED Talk. I'm talking about two things you already carry with you every day and probably don't give enough credit to:

1. Your gut
2. Your grit

You're sitting on a decision making toolkit so powerful it's a wonder we still doubt ourselves. But we do, constantly.

We act like the answers are always "out there" in a course, a consultant, a podcast, or a playbook. Most of the time, the tools are already *inside of you*.

Let's break them down.

### *1. GUT*

Your gut is your internal compass. It's the feeling you get when something's off, even if you can't explain why. It's also the fire you feel when something just clicks.

Let's be clear: Gut instinct doesn't mean guessing. It means *pattern recognition + experience + subconscious logic* firing quickly.

You've been building this tool since childhood, through wins, mistakes, relationships, jobs, and side hustles.

But here's the problem: We've been trained to ignore our gut in favour of "facts." We overanalyse and spreadsheet ourselves into oblivion.

And guess what? The spreadsheet might say *yes*, but your gut is screaming *run*. That's not woo-woo, it's wisdom.

### How to Strengthen Your Gut:

- Review past decisions: When did you ignore your gut and regret it?
- Pay attention to physical cues: Tension, ease, energy, dread.
- Give it language: "This feels right…." (your gut doesn't need to be mysterious).

## *2. GRIT*

Anyone can make a decision on Day 1. Grit is what gets you to Day 58 when nothing's going right and you haven't slept and your "clever idea" is starting to look like an expensive mistake.

Grit is your ability to keep going when things suck. It's the part of you that:

- Keeps emailing when no one replies.
- Shows up to the 8am client call even though it's the last thing you feel like doing.
- Sends the invoice. Chases the invoice. Sends it again.
- Adjusts, adapts, figures things out as you go.

Here's what people get wrong: Grit doesn't mean burning out or "hustling harder." It means staying committed to the decision you made long enough to see what it's capable of becoming.

### How to Strengthen Your Grit:

- Break big goals into tiny tasks (and do them).
- Keep showing up, especially on the days you don't want to.
- Learn to sit with discomfort without self-destructing.

## You Already Have What You Need

You don't need another think tank to tell you what your gut already knows. You don't need a certificate to tell you you're gritty.

You're ready. You're equipped. You've got the tools.

## Final Word

The best decisions aren't made with perfect data or divine insight. They're made by people who trust their gut, show up with grit, and use every tool available.

Next time you feel stuck or not ready, ask yourself: "Do I *really* not know what to do? or am I just ignoring what I already know and feel?

The answer is usually closer than you think. It's in your gut.

# Chapter 5

## FEAR—the Real Boss Behind Your Bad Decisions

**FEAR RARELY SAYS, 'I'M SCARED.' IT USUALLY SAYS, 'BE PRACTICAL.'**

## The Silent CEO Running Your Life Until You Say "F*** It"

Let's stop sugarcoating it. Sometimes, you're not stuck because of time, resources, or the market. You're stuck because of **fear**.

Fear is the real decision-maker behind so many non-decisions. It's the internal committee that vetoes every bold move with questions like:

- "What if I fail?"
- "What if people judge me?"
- "What if I don't know what I'm doing?"
- "What if I waste my time/money/reputation?"

And so, we stall. And stall. And stall.

Here's the thing:  Sometimes **Fear** shows up dressed as logic, or caution, or the classic: "Let me just wait until the timing's better."

## Fear Isn't the Problem. Avoiding It Is.

The truth is, fear itself isn't bad. It has a purpose. It's useful, keeps you alive, and stops you from touching hot stoves, or replying "sure" to things you can't afford.

The problem lies in how we manage our lives to avoid fear, instead of building the courage to move with it.

Here's the truth:

The moment you step into anything meaningful, you'll feel fear. This will make you feel exposed, unsure, shaky, and unqualified.

This is the exact point where most of us say, "No thanks. Maybe next year," but not all. Some of us feel the fear and say, "F*** it. Let's go anyway."

## Fear's Greatest Trick: Making You Think You're Being Smart

Fear loves to convince you that you're just being "careful." It whispers stuff like:

- "Maybe you need more time."
- "You should probably ask three more people first."
- "Don't rush there's no need to take unnecessary risks."

Does this sound familiar? None of these thoughts are outright wrong. But all of them, if left unchallenged, lead to the same place: Nothing happening. And the longer you delay, the more fear starts to own your future.

## Risk vs. Regret

You've probably heard the quote:

**"Risk Is Better Than Regret."**

Read that again.

You can survive risk. You can learn from it. You can pivot, adapt, recover, and grow. But regret?

Regret is what happens when you chose fear again and again—until, one day, you realise you've built a career, or a life based on *avoidance* instead of *action*.

Risk is a moment. Regret is a slow burn.

You won't remember all the things that didn't go to plan. But you'll absolutely remember the big things you never had the guts to try.

## The Science of Fear

Fear has a job. It's designed to protect you. It's part of your brain's operating system that says: "Hey, this feels unfamiliar or dangerous. Stop."

But here's the thing: The brain doesn't know the difference between "dangerous" and "uncomfortable."

A study by neuroscientists Raymundo Báez-Mendoza (German Primate Centre) and Fabian Grabenhorst (University of Oxford) found that neurons in the amygdala don't just react to fear or danger, they also track the probability, size, and uncertainty of rewards.

In other words, the same brain region that tells you to run from a threat is also busy calculating whether your latest business idea is worth the risk.

So:

- Starting a business = same fear signal as running from a bear.
- Quitting your job = same signal as jumping into traffic.

Discomfort isn't a signal to stop; it's a sign you're stretching. Growth doesn't come from comfort zones; it comes from pressure, challenge, and pushing past your limits.

Ask any professional athlete during preseason. They'll tell you that it's the discomfort that builds champions.

## Your "F*** It" Moment Is the Break Point

Fear will always be part of the process. You don't overcome it with enough planning or motivational quotes. What you *do* is override it. And that usually sounds like: "F*** it. I'd rather try and fail than keep wondering."

That's when fear loses its grip. Not because it disappears, but because it no longer gets to control your life.

## How to Recognise Fear in Disguise

Here are some **Phrases** dressed up as logic:

| What You Say | What Fear Means |
|---|---|
| "I just want to be fully ready first." | I'm scared I won't be perfect. |
| "It's not the right time." | I'm scared I'll look stupid. |
| "I don't have enough experience." | I'm scared of being exposed. |
| "What if people think I'm not legit?" | I'm scared of judgement. |
| "Let me just think on it a bit more." | I'm scared to commit and take responsibility. |

Fear always wants to be in control. But guess what? It only wins if you let it.

## Final Word

*Courage Isn't Confidence*

You don't need to be fearless to move, you just need to be willing to move *with fear in the room.* Courage is doing it while you're still unsure. It's saying: "Risk is better than regret." Because it is.

Say the words. Make the move. Let fear come with you—you take control.

# Chapter 6

## The Myth of Perfect Timing

**THERE'S NO SUCH THING AS THE RIGHT TIME, JUST THE RIGHT AMOUNT OF COURAGE.**

# Nobody Knows When the "Right Time" Is

Let's get one thing straight: "I'm just waiting for the right time" is almost always code for "I'm scared and procrastinating, but I want to sound strategic."

We've all said it. And we've all believed it, even as the right time conveniently keeps shifting further into the future, like your mate who's five minutes away, but hasn't left the house yet (yes, John I'm referring to you).

Perfect timing is a myth. It doesn't exist and it never has. Trust me, the people who do big things, start companies, quit jobs, launch offers, change direction, didn't do it because the stars aligned, they did it because they decided that **now** was good enough.

## What Does "Perfect Timing" Even Mean?

Most people never define it. They just wait for:

- More money
- More certainty
- Fewer responsibilities
- Better market conditions

The problem is, life doesn't hand you the perfect opportunity with no distractions, no risk, and no reason to hesitate.

There's always something: Kids. Rent. The market.

Your boss. Your confidence. The economy. The dog's birthday.

There is no such thing as a quiet moment where everything is lined up perfectly and someone says, "NOW. GO. THIS IS YOUR WINDOW."

That moment is too rare and it's usually impossible to identify.

## Timing *Is* a Factor But Not a Strategy

Let's be fair: timing matters. But it matters *in motion*. Not in theory. Good timing can make something easier but it's not the *reason* you succeed—commitment is.

The people who build things don't wait for permission, they act, and *then* they adjust to the timing they're in. They start messy, course-correct, and use gut and grit.

Waiting for perfect timing is just a clever way to delay making a real decision.

## The Cost of Waiting

Every time you delay something because "it's not the right time," you're incurring a hidden cost:

- Missed momentum
- Missed learning
- Missed relationships
- Missed income

We like to think that pausing means we're "holding steady," but time doesn't freeze; the world keeps moving. You don't feel it at first, and then six months down the line, you're further away than when you started.

Progress punishes hesitation.

## Here's a Wild Thought: What If Now IS Exactly the Right Time?

What if the discomfort you feel isn't a warning sign but a signal you're on the edge of growth? What if waiting until you "feel ready" is like waiting until you're "fit enough" to go to the gym?

You don't become more ready by waiting, only by *starting*. Ready isn't a feeling. It's the result of moving before you're 100% sure of the outcome.

## Quick Reality Checks (AKA Timing Lies We Tell Ourselves)

| What You Say | What's Really Happening |
|---|---|
| "I'll start when I have more time." | You'll never have more time, only different excuses. |
| "I'm just too busy right now." | You're always busy. If not now, then when? |
| "The market isn't great." | The market is always volatile. Ask any founder. |
| "I'll wait until I'm 100% confident." | That's not how confidence works. It follows action. |
| "Maybe next quarter/year/month." | You're hiding. Own it. Or move. |

## Final Word

There is no "perfect time." There's only **now**, and what you choose to do with it. The people who win stop waiting and start building even if it's scary.

Even if it's Tuesday and we are out of coffee. Progress doesn't care about your timing. It rewards your decision. If you've been waiting for a sign, this is it.

Say, "F*** It. Now is good enough."

# Chapter 7

## Action Is the Answer (Even When It's the Wrong One)

**YOU CAN'T THINK YOUR WAY INTO CLARITY. YOU HAVE TO MOVE YOUR WAY THERE.**

## The Best Way to Figure Things Out Is to Start. Trial. Error. Repeat.

Let's just say it: Most of us don't need more time to think. We need to *move our ass*. You're confused because you're trying to solve the whole thing first in your head.

**My suggestion is to give it some thought but then, DO something. Action > Analysis**

Here's the simple equation:

Action = Data.

Inaction = Guessing.

Until you make a move, everything you think is just a theory. The minute you act, even if it's slightly wrong you've got something to respond to:

- Real-world feedback
- New inputs
- Actual progress

You don't need to be right, you just need to be in motion.

## What If I Get It Wrong?

If you are like me and many others, you most likely will. You will launch the wrong product, hire the wrong person, send the wrong email, pitch to the wrong client, buy the wrong tech, or say the wrong thing on a call and then replay it in your head at 2am.

Wrong action still moves you forward faster than perfect planning because now you know. Knowing beats wondering every single time. Failure is feedback that promotes growth, whereas inaction gives you nothing more than regret.

## Every Win Starts Ugly

Behind every "success story", there's a highlight reel that skips over the awkward stuff:

- The failed launch
- The client that ghosted
- The days you sat frozen in front of your laptop, uncertain if it was decision fatigue, burnout, or just another quiet crisis of purpose.

No one posts that part on LinkedIn. But that's where the real business, clarity, and growth happen. Success doesn't come from nailing it on the first try. It comes from making so many tries that failure stops scaring you.

## You Can't Steer a Parked Car

Want to know why you feel stuck? Because you're sitting still, trying to *think* your way into confidence. But clarity doesn't come from sitting still, it comes from traction.

You don't get direction *before* you act. You get direction *by* acting. You don't need to know the full path, just take the next step.

***Try → Learn → Adjust → Repeat***

Let's keep it simple.

| Step | What it Looks Like |
|---|---|
| Try | Launch the thing. Start the convo. Hit send. |
| Learn | See what lands. What worked. What flopped. |
| Adjust | Tweak. Pivot. Rethink. Improve. |
| Repeat | Go again. Stronger. Smarter. Faster. |

This loop is how every great business, brand, and leader is built—not through flawless execution, but momentum.

## Action Cures More Than You Think

- Feeling unmotivated? → Action sparks motivation.
- Feeling unsure? → Action gives clarity.
- Feeling stuck? → Action shakes you loose.
- Feeling afraid? → Action proves you can handle it.

The secret isn't confidence; it's evidence, and the only way to build evidence is by doing something.

## Final Word

You don't need to feel ready. You don't need a full plan. You don't even need to be totally sure it's the right move. You just need to act.

Movement leads to insight and clarity lives on the other side of that first step. Even if it's the wrong move, it's better than no move.

"F*** it. Let's go."

# Chapter 8

## Decisions Make You

**YOU BUILD YOURSELF BY ONE BOLD DECISION AT A TIME.**

## Your Life Isn't Shaped By What You Hoped For— It's Shaped By What You *Choose*

You don't become who you are because of your background, your job title, or your LinkedIn headline.

You become who you are based on every decision you make. Every bold move. Every "F*** It" moment. Every messy action you took when clarity wasn't there yet.

## You Are the Product of Your Calls

Look back. You didn't get to where you are by *waiting*, you got here by:

- Saying yes to something new.
- Saying no to something that drained you.
- Quitting when it wasn't working.
- Starting when you weren't ready.
- Hiring, firing, launching, pivoting before it all made sense.

And you probably made a few calls that went sideways, but here's the plot twist: It's not just the good decisions that make you, but the ownership of all of them—the good, bad, delayed, and impulsive.

Taking ownership is how you grow and growth is the whole point.

## You Don't Need to Get It All Right. Just Get Moving.

There's no prize for perfect decision making. There's no trophy for "least mistakes made." There *is* power in becoming the kind of person who:

- Makes the call.
- Backs themselves.
- Stands by the decision or learns fast and adjusts.

That's leadership. That's maturity. That's self-trust in action.

You don't need to be right all the time, but you do need to be engaged, in motion and on the field to score the goal.

## The Decisions You Don't Make Still Shape You

Let's flip it. It's not just the decisions you made that define you, it's the ones you *didn't* make.

- The thing you never launched.
- The conversation you avoided.
- The exit you postponed.
- The idea you shelved for "later."
- The role, business, or dream you quietly let drift.

Those choices still shaped you, but in a way that shrunk your world instead of expanding it.

## Want a Bigger Life?
## Make Bigger Decisions.

This isn't a hustle culture manifesto. This is a reminder that your next evolution is waiting behind your next decision. Not your next goal. Not your next plan. Not your next big "aha." Your next **decision**.

- Do I stay or go?
- Say yes or no?
- Launch or wait?
- Speak up or stay safe?
- Let it slide or draw the line?

Every decision is a declaration of who you are and what you value.

Want more momentum? Choose.

Want more peace? Choose.

Want more opportunity, growth, and meaning? Choose.

## Final Word

*It was Never About Being Sure—it was About Being Brave*. No one has all the answers and no one knows for sure. Anyone who acts like they do is either lying or selling something.

You don't need perfect knowledge, you just need **courage** because courage compounds. As decisions do, over time.

If you become the person who acts, builds and backs themselves, you become someone you can trust. That, more than anything else, is what makes you unstoppable.

# Chapter 9

## Manifesting Is Great, but It Doesn't Work Without Taking Action

**MANIFEST IT ALL YOU WANT, THE UNIVERSE STILL EXPECTS YOU TO TAKE ACTION.**

## You Can't Just Visualise a Better Life—You Have to Choose One

Let's talk about manifesting. Yes, that thing where you write your dreams on sticky notes, light candles, speak to the Universe, and then wait for someone to knock on the door to deliver magic.

And listen, I love a good vision board, and have been using them for years, but let's get something straight: You can't "think" your way into a better life, you have to *choose* your way into it.

Manifesting without action is just spiritual procrastination. It's like dressing up for a marathon and then waiting for the finish line to come to *you*.

We've glamorised the idea that if you think positively enough, you can attract anything. Do you know what *actually* attracts opportunity?

- Showing up.
- Sending the email.
- Calling the client.
- Posting the thing.
- Making the decision.

Manifesting can help you set direction, but if you're not pairing it with deliberate, uncomfortable, consistent action, you're not manifesting, you're just journaling.

# The Universe Isn't Ghosting You

People love to say, "The Universe has my back." Great. But the Universe also likes it when you **do your damn job.**

Guess what? The job of building a better life includes:

- Making decisions you're scared to make.
- Risking being seen (and judged).
- Choosing progress over perfection.
- Backing yourself before you feel ready.
- Showing up *before* the confidence hits.

Manifesting your dream life while avoiding your responsibilities is the equivalent of praying for a harvest but never planting a seed.

***Manifesting + Action = Power***

***Manifesting + Avoidance = Fantasy***

Visualisation is useful and believing for something matters along with focusing on what you want, but such habits work in service of action, not instead of it.

Let's break it down:

## What Manifesting Does

- Clarifies your goals
- Sharpens your intention
- Keeps you focused
- Builds optimism

## What Manifesting Doesn't Do

- Make decisions for you
- Do the hard or boring bits
- Overcome fear of failure
- Handle rejection, discomfort, or doubt

The Universe moves with you, not *for* you.

## Final Word

You can light your candle, write your affirmations, and visualise your future self in a beachfront villa sipping iced oat lattes after your thriving launch, but to get there you need to *Take Action*.

Make the call. Post the video. Say yes. Say no.

Make the decision your future self is *waiting* for.
The Universe might be listening, but you're the one holding the pen. Manifest it, sure. But also, do the work that is needed.

# Chapter 10

## What Would You Do if You Weren't Scared (or Tired or Broke)?

**FEAR, FATIGUE, AND FINANCES AREN'T THE END, THEY'RE JUST THE FIRST THREE EXCUSES TO BEAT.**

## Decision Making When Everything Feels Heavy.

Most people don't realise this, but their decisions are being made by their current state, not their actual potential.

They say no to something not because it's a bad idea, but because they're:

- Exhausted
- Financially stressed
- Overwhelmed
- Scared
- Burned out
- Distracted
- Unsure

Which is fair because those are real constraints. But here's the trap: if you only make decisions based on your current capacity, you'll keep rebuilding the life you already have, not the one you *actually* want.

## The Wrong CEO is Running the Show

Imagine you've got a "Future You" and a "Right Now You."

- **Future You** wants clarity, freedom, confidence, and more income.
- **Right-now You** is in survival mode and just wants to nap.

Guess who keeps making the decisions? Right-now You. The one with the lowest energy and the most fear.

It's like letting your most tired, emotionally unstable employee set your entire strategy. No wonder everything feels hard.

## Your Circumstances Shouldn't Dictate Your Choices

Let's say you're broke. Of course, you feel like you can't take a risk. Of course you want safety. But ask yourself, "What decision would I make if I trusted that I could figure it out?" and then, "What would I choose now if I knew I'd get the energy, money, and clarity later?"

Here's the trick: **Your resources expand when your commitment does.**

Not before.

## Don't Let a Temporary State Create a Permanent Stagnation

Being tired, broke, scared is temporary, but the decisions you make in that state can unconsciously shape years of your life.

A lot of people spend years stuck because they made one decision when they were exhausted and told themselves it was "safe."

They quit their business idea, stayed in the wrong job, said *no* to a big opportunity and *downsized* their dream before it even started. All of this happening because they assumed today's energy level was permanent.

## Make the Decision—Then Solve the Problem

The secret?

***Decide First. Solve Later.***

You can say yes to the opportunity, and then figure out how you'll deliver.

You can book the flight, and then sort out the finances.

When you say no to the wrong thing, you trust the right thing will appear. Set the date and become the person who's ready by then.

Every entrepreneur, founder, or creator who's done anything meaningful made decisions they had no business making. Yet, they made the call, *then rose to meet it.*

### Burn the Boats.

There's an old story I always come back to.

Alexander the Great landed on foreign soil with his army, knowing full well that what lay ahead was dangerous and uncertain. Once they reached the shore, he didn't hesitate. He gave a clear order: destroy the ships they'd arrived in.

No safety net.
No plan B.
No way back.

By removing the option to retreat, he forced absolute commitment. His men weren't fighting with one foot out the door anymore. Their focus shifted instantly. Survival, progress, and victory became the only things that mattered.

And that idea still works today.

Sometimes the reason we stall isn't lack of talent, opportunity, or drive, it's because we leave ourselves an escape route. We keep the door cracked open "just in case." Just in case it gets hard. Just in case it doesn't work. Just in case we get uncomfortable.

Burning the boats is about deciding that turning back is no longer an option. When you remove every distraction, every fallback, every excuse, your energy locks onto what's right in front of you.

That's when real progress happens.
That's when pressure turns into clarity.
That's when you find out what you're actually capable of.

Sometimes the only way forward... is to make sure there's no way back.

## Ask the Better Question

Next time you feel stuck, don't ask:

- "Can I afford it?"
- "Am I ready?"
- "What if I fail?"
- "Will people get it?"
- "Is this smart right now?"

Instead, ask:

- "What would I choose if I trusted myself more than I feared this?"
- "What would future me thank me for?"
- "What would I do if I weren't scared, tired, or broke?"

## Final Word

Most people build a life around their limits. The people who move, create, and evolve build a life around their visions, and then stretch themselves to catch up.

Stop asking your fear to set your direction. Instead, ask your future, "What do you need me to choose today?"

Then back yourself, not because you're ready, but because *you're willing to grow into it.*

# Chapter 11

## Courage Doesn't Need a Committee

**ADVICE IS HELPFUL, BUT AT SOME POINT, THE BRAVEST THING YOU CAN DO IS STOP ASKING AND START ACTING.**

## Stop Asking People Who've Never Done It

Let's talk about advice, or more specifically, the *advice-seeking spiral*. You know the one.

You have an idea, feel a pull and you're 80% sure you want to go for it, but then you start asking around for other people's opinions:

- "What do you think?"
- "Am I crazy?"
- "Would you do it?"

And just like that, you've handed your dream to a group chat.

## The Hidden Problem with "Just Asking Around"

It feels smart. Responsible. Even strategic but actually you're scared and you're hoping someone else will take responsibility for the risk.

Does these sound familiar:

- "I'm just getting a few opinions."
- "It's good to get different perspectives."
- "I'm being thorough."

Let's call it what it is: Crowdsourcing your courage while looking for someone else to say, "Yes, go for it, and if it fails, I'll take the blame."

Here's the truth. No one can do the brave part *for you.*

## Stop Asking People Who *Aren't* Where You Want To Be

The internet is full of people who have opinions but no experience in your field or real investment in your life.

Don't ask your cousin who's never run a business if you should quit your job.

Don't ask your coworker who hates risk if you should raise your prices.

Don't ask someone who's never taken a leap if you should take yours. Their advice isn't coming from your potential—it's coming from *their fear.*

If you crowdsource your courage, you'll always default to the most cautious voice in the room.

And guess what? Cautious voices are *loud*, especially when they're unqualified.

Let's be clear, advice is valuable. But only when it's specific, intentional, and from the right people. Most of the time people aren't looking for advice—they're looking for **permission**.

A few signs you're stalling behind advice-seeking:

- You've already made up your mind but keep "asking around"
- You say, "I'm just waiting for a few more opinions" (for the 7th time)

- You ask people who've never done what you're considering
- You downplay your idea so it's "easier to accept"
- You get mad when someone says, "Yeah, go for it"

All signs point to this: You're not looking for advice; you're looking for a way out of the decision. You've done the work. You've thought it through. You've weighed the risks.

At this point, asking more people isn't about getting clarity. It's about outsourcing the discomfort of deciding. But discomfort is part of the process. Growth isn't a consensus. It's a decision. And if you feel it in your gut, that's enough.

## Final Word

You don't need a committee. You don't need consensus. You don't need everyone to nod and clap before you leap. You just need to know what *you* want and then back yourself.

So, here's your new rule:

Ask fewer people. Trust yourself more. And never hand your decision to someone who doesn't have to live with the consequences.

Courage is not something you get from others; it's something you activate in yourself when you finally stop asking and make a decision.

# Chapter 12

## Confidence Comes After

THE BRAVEST PEOPLE RARELY FEEL READY; THEY JUST MOVE ANYWAY AND CONFIDENCE CATCHES UP.

## Confidence Is Not a Prerequisite—It's a Result

You don't get confident *before* you do the thing; you get confident *by doing it* awkwardly, nervously, with shaking hands and a pounding chest.

It's like expecting to be fluent in another language before ever speaking it out loud. Nope. You're going to mess it up. Get laughed at and then *get better*. That's how confidence is built.

## Confidence is a Muscle

We treat confidence like a magical feeling that some people just *have*. "She's just naturally confident." "He always seems so sure of himself." "They're fearless."

These are all lies. What they *have* in common is repetition. They've repeatedly made decisions, taken risks, and screwed up.

They've learned, improved, and repeated the process again and again. Confidence isn't natural—it's earned.

It's the compound interest of discomfort. Most people avoid the discipline it takes to build confidence.

How many things have you delayed, avoided, or talked yourself out of because you "didn't feel confident yet?"

- Speaking up
- Starting the business
- Posting the content

- Asking for the sale
- Changing careers
- Raising your rates
- Calling the client back
- Launching the thing

There are many moments where you had enough skill but not enough *nerve*, because deep down you were waiting for a feeling that was never coming.

Confidence doesn't show up to help you decide. It shows up to celebrate that you already did.

## Confidence Follows Commitment

The moment you commit, truly commit; things change. Commitment triggers creativity. It kills excuses and *pulls confidence forward* like a magnet.

You become more confident when you're already in motion, not while you're thinking about it from your couch.

## Yes, It's Supposed to Feel Scary

Your nervous system hates change. It's not trying to ruin your life; it's trying to protect you. It doesn't know the difference between,

- Launching a product
- Asking someone on a date
- Starting a podcast

- Or being chased by a bear

All it sees is *uncertainty* and starts sweating. That's not a sign to stop, it's a sign you're stretching. That's exactly where confidence is built—*not in the safe zone, but in the stretch zone*.

## The Confidence Loop

| Step | What Happens |
|---|---|
| Take Action | You do something before you're ready. |
| Survive it | It wasn't perfect, but it wasn't fatal. |
| Learn Something | You gain insight. Skill. Self-trust. |
| Repeat it | You do it again, but this time with 5% more swagger. |
| Feel Capable | That's confidence. Not cockiness. Just a quiet "Hey, I've got this." |

It doesn't have to be huge. One scary decision. One uncomfortable conversation. One brave move. That's how you become the confident version of you. One decision at a time.

## Final Word

Confidence isn't something you find but something you become through repeated exposure to your own power.

If you're sitting around waiting for the confidence to start, you've got it backwards. Confidence doesn't power the decision; the decision powers the confidence.

Choose first. Move second. And watch confidence catch up.

# Chapter 13

## The 24-Hour Rule

**IF YOU CAN'T DECIDE IN 24 HOURS, IT'S NOT BECAUSE YOU DON'T KNOW, IT'S BECAUSE YOU DON'T WANT TO OWN IT.**

## You Don't Need More Time To Make That Decision—You Need a Deadline

Most people think they're being thoughtful when they delay decisions. They say things like:

- "I just want to sleep on it."
- "Let me sit with this for a bit."
- "I'll make a call next week."
- "I want to be sure."

Sounds wise, right? Nope, it's just procrastination dressed differently.

### Time Isn't the Problem. Fear Is.

If you're being real, you already know what you want to do, but you're just scared of the consequences.

Scared it'll flop. Scared it'll work. Scared someone won't like it. Scared of committing. Scared you'll look stupid.

So instead of deciding, you spiral. You re-read the email 14 times. You open the same tab every morning like it's changed. You ask three more people what they'd do. You lose a week, or a month, or a golden opportunity.

Not because you're not ready, but because you didn't give yourself a line in the sand.

## Enter: The 24-Hour Rule

It's stupidly simple: Give yourself 24 hours to make the decision. One day. That's it.

- 24 hours to weigh it.
- 24 hours to research it.
- 24 hours to trust your gut.

Then hit send. Pick up the phone. Say yes. Say no. Make the damn call.

**Why This Works? Because time isn't the real problem, it's uncertainty fatigue.** The longer a decision lingers, the heavier it gets.

You start attaching emotion to it. Then identity. Then imagined consequences until suddenly you're questioning your whole personality.

Small decisions get big when you let them rot in your inbox. The 24-Hour Rule kills the rot and gives you *just enough* time to be thoughtful, but not enough time to spiral.

## It's Not About Perfection. It's About Momentum

You will still make some bad calls. You will still second-guess yourself sometimes. But you'll also move. And that movement will teach you more than a month of overthinking ever could.

The point isn't to get every decision right, it's to keep deciding, learning, and evolving. That's how you grow—not in loops, but in leaps.

## Final Word

Most of your best decisions are waiting on the other side of a 24-hour promise: "I will not be thinking about this next week. I'll know by tomorrow."

No committee. No delay. Just a decision.

# Chapter 14

## No One Knows What They're Doing, They're Just Doing It Anyway

**CLARITY IS OPTIONAL—
MOVEMENT IS NOT.**

## We're All Making It Up. Some People Are Just Louder About It

Here's a thought: Every confident person you know is winging it at least 40% of the time. Some are closer to 80%, but they hide it behind sharp outfits and loud opinions. (Ok, no scientific research here, just my 30 years in business management talking).

Welcome to the big secret of adulthood, entrepreneurship, leadership, and *basically everything past Year 10 … No one really knows what the hell they're doing.* We're all just going for it.

## The Lie We All Believed

Somewhere along the line, you were told that real adults, leaders, and founders have it all figured out.

They know the plan. They know the risks. They know exactly how to handle any situation with calm, poise, and the right font on their pitch deck.

Let me be clear: That person doesn't exist. Or if they do, they're probably terrifying at parties.

The rest of us are winging it, Googling acronyms mid-meeting, rewriting emails five times, and nodding seriously while internally panicking.

## It's not imposter syndrome.
## It's called, being human.

Imposter syndrome doesn't show up because you're unqualified, it shows up because you care. Because you're growing. Because you're in the deep end and actually *trying*.

We all act like we're the only ones doubting ourselves. So, here's the truth: You don't need to feel certain to be credible. You don't need to feel confident to be capable. You just need to act, while scared, confused, and slightly over-caffeinated.

Humbly, let me say this: the people you admire aren't more qualified, they're just braver about showing their mess.

- They start before they're ready.
- They post before the website is perfect.
- They say, "Here's what I think...," and then adjust later if they're wrong.

They don't *have* confidence, they manufacture it through action; and people believe them, not because they're perfect, but because they *go first*.

## The Real Skill—Looking Like You Know What You're Doing While Learning on the Job

Honestly, that's the whole game. Speak like you know, but Google like you don't. Walk into the room, even if your knees are shaking.

Take the meeting, even if your calendar says, "don't do it." Say yes to the client, then figure it out at 11:48pm with YouTube tutorials. You don't need to fake it you just need to *move through it*. Because clarity comes through motion.

## Final Word

Stop waiting to feel "qualified." Stop assuming you're the only one sweating. Everyone's guessing. Everyone's bluffing. Everyone's doing their best impression of someone who knows what's going on.

The ones who move ahead are just the ones who decide anyway. So, stop disqualifying yourself. Say YES and START moving.

You're just as "qualified" as anyone else pretending not to be pretending.

# Chapter 15

## You Can Always Change Your Mind

**DECIDING DOESN'T MEAN YOU'RE LOCKED IN, IT JUST MEANS YOU'VE STARTED.**

## Most Decisions Aren't Permanent—You're Just Treating Them Like They Are

Let's clear something up: Commitment doesn't mean you've locked yourself in a burning building with no exit, and growth doesn't mean *getting it right the first time*.

You can decide. And you can back yourself and still change direction later with your head high. Changing your mind isn't a failure. It's a skill.

## People Treat Every Decision Like a Marriage

### *(But Most Are Just Dates)*

We over-dramatise decisions like:

- What offer to launch
- What title to use
- What business name to pick
- What platform to build on
- What niche to target
- What job to say yes to

But the reality is that most of our decisions are *reversible*, or at least *tweakable*. You're allowed to shift, reassess, and redirect. That's not inconsistency, it's strategic evolution.

## The Difference between Fear-based Flip-Flopping and Strategic Shifting

There's a *wrong* way to change your mind. You don't get to abandon your goals every time it gets hard and call it "alignment." You don't get to half-commit to something, panic, and call it "pivoting." That's just quitting.

But if you've tried something with intention, given it enough time to learn, and realised it's not aligned anymore, then yes, you can change direction. That's not failure, that's feedback.

## Real Decision Makers Course-Correct

You know what indecision usually sounds like?

- "I just don't want to make the wrong move..."
- "What if I regret it later?"
- "I don't want to waste time."

But guess what's worse than the wrong move? **No Move.** You can fix the wrong move. You can adjust, and reset, but you can't build anything on *stalling.*

You're allowed to make real-time updates. Just because you picked something at one point in time doesn't mean it still fits now. You grow. Your market grows. Your confidence grows.

What felt bold two years ago might feel boring now. What scared you before might excite you now. And, what felt right *then* might not feel right *next*.

That's not being inconsistent, that's being awake and alert to the direction you are moving in.

## Final Word

Don't use "you can always change your mind" as an excuse to stay non-committal forever. That's avoidance.

But also, don't let the fear of being "wrong" keep you stuck in what no longer works. Decide boldly, learn fast, and adjust smart.

You're not here to be perfect. You're here to be in motion, in tune, and in charge. That means making the best decision you can today and making a better one tomorrow.

# Chapter 16

## Memento Mori

**MEMENTO MORI ISN'T ABOUT OBSESSING OVER DEATH, IT'S ABOUT GETTING SERIOUS ABOUT LIFE.**

# You're Not Running Out of Options. You're Running Out of Time and That's the Whole Point

Let's clear something up: "F*** It" isn't reckless. It's not lazy. It's not giving up. "F*** It" is *remembering what matters when fear, fatigue, or perfection are trying to take over.* It's a gut-level reminder that you're not here forever, so why keep putting off what you want?

That's the core of **Memento Mori**; a Latin phase borrowed from the Stoics. It means: "Remember you will die." Not in a terrifying way, "let's go cry on a friend's shoulder", but in a "get your priorities straight" kind of way.

## Why You Need This Reminder

We think we've got time. Time to circle back. Time to play it safe. Time to keep the "I will do it one day" dream on the shelf.

But you don't have forever and when you remember that *your whole decision-making framework shifts.*

Suddenly, "someday" starts sounding like a scam, and "maybe later" feels like a gamble with odds you didn't mean to take. Memento Mori strips the bullshit away.

It asks: "If this was your last year, would you still keep waiting?"

## The Intersection of F*** It and Decisiveness

That moment when you say "F*** It" and just go for it is not impulsive, it's clarity—the kind most people are too distracted to access.

It's the mental switch that flips when you stop assuming there's always more time to figure it out.

- You hit publish.
- You make the call.
- You leave the thing that's slowly draining you.
- You finally back yourself, not because you're ready, but because *you're awake*.

"F*** it" isn't careless. It's decisive and it's *intentional urgency*.

## You Don't Need More Time. You Need Fewer Excuses.

This isn't a productivity hack, it's perspective. The real issue isn't grinding harder but being clear on what *truly* matters before your time gets spent on stuff that never did.

The client you hate working with ... let them go.

The opportunity that scares you ... say yes.

The idea that's been living in your note's app for three years ... launch it.

Act like your time means something. Because it does.

## The Purpose of Memento Mori is Not to Frighten, But to Inspire Action.

Embracing Memento Mori is not about living in fear of death, but about living fully aware of the gift of being alive.

It's about asking:

- "Is this decision building the life I actually want?"
- "Would future me thank me for this?"
- "Am I putting this off for a reason or out of fear?"

You just need a reason that beats your fear ... and the best reason? You're here. You're alive. And you've got this one shot to get it right for you.

## Final Word

Memento Mori is your daily reminder, that life won't wait and the perfect moment doesn't exist. The time to act is now. Say "F*** It" and make it count.

# Chapter 17

## F*** It, I'm Having a Cold Shower

**DISCOMFORT DOESN'T KILL YOU.
AVOIDING IT SLOWLY DOES.**

## Let's Talk About Cold Showers

Not because they're trendy. Not because Wim Hof said so (even though, yes, he's a legend), because they're the perfect metaphor for what most of us need to face: We're getting way too comfortable and it's making us weak.

Now, before you roll your eyes, PLEASE hear me out.

## How It Started

A few years ago, I read about Wim Hof, this wild Dutch guy doing breathwork and plunging himself into freezing rivers like it was a casual Tuesday. He wasn't doing it for likes. He was doing it to reset the body, boost the immune system, and train the mind.

So, I gave it a go and the first cold shower was brutal. Yep, I swore. I negotiated with myself in real time. But I did it.

The next day, I did it again. Not because I wanted to but because I said: **"F*** it. Let's go."**

Now, I jump into a cold shower *in winter* like it's nothing. No drama. No buildup. Just in, done, move on.

## Why It Matters

The cold doesn't just refresh your body, it recalibrates your mind. It reminds you that you can handle discomfort and that most of what you avoid isn't dangerous, it's just *unpleasant*.

And guess what? Most of the goals you're chasing live on the other side of something slightly unpleasant.

- Waking up early
- Saying no to sugar
- Going to the gym
- Having a hard conversation
- Raising your prices
- Taking a risk
- Letting someone down so you don't let yourself down

All of it is uncomfortable. But not impossible.

## Comfort Is the Real Enemy

Modern life has made it ridiculously easy to avoid anything unpleasant:

- Climate-controlled homes
- Heated seats
- Food on demand
- Motivational podcasts that delay actual action

We've gotten so soft we think *mild effort* is pain. But when you practice choosing discomfort, even in small doses, something shifts.

You stop negotiating with yourself. You stop needing

everything to feel "right." You stop waiting for motivation and start building momentum.

"F*** It" isn't just a phrase, it's the launch button for resilience.

## The Mental Reps That Build You

That cold shower isn't just about the water, it's a daily rep in doing the hard thing. And the more you do it, the more it bleeds into other areas of your life:

- You become harder to shake.
- You recover faster from stress.
- You trust yourself more.

You realise: "If I can do that, I can do this too." That's how resilience is built.

## Final Word

Cold showers taught me something success never did: You don't need to feel ready to take control, you just need to stop hesitating.

Comfort breeds delay, discomfort breeds discipline, and the only thing standing between the two is usually a single decision.

Next time your brain tries to negotiate you out of something hard, uncomfortable, or inconvenient ... Don't wait. Don't spiral.

Just say, "F*** It". And move.

# Final Words

## I leave you with this—
## "F*** It" Was the Beginning

**"F*** IT" IS THE BEGINNING OF MOMENTUM.**

You probably thought your *"F*** It"* moment was reckless. It wasn't. It was the beginning of momentum. The moment you stopped outsourcing your potential. The split-second where you decided that fear doesn't get the final vote.

"F*** It" wasn't you giving up. It was you *finally showing up*. You weren't being careless; you were being brave in a way that didn't need permission.

## "F*** It" was the Beginning Of ...

- Saying yes to something that scared you.
- Saying no to something that drained you.
- Backing yourself without a 10-step PowerPoint.
- Trusting your gut even if it shook a little.
- Letting go of *how it's supposed to look.*
- Doing it anyway.

Sure, maybe you didn't have the plan, but you had courage and you followed it.

That's leadership. That's growth. That's how lives change—not in perfect timing, but in *imperfect action.*

## What Happens After "F*** It"?

You become someone new. Someone who moves. Someone who adapts. Someone who *decides.*

Not because it's easy, but because the cost of regret is louder than the voice of doubt.

And maybe everything didn't go according to plan, but maybe that's the best part, because now, you're living a life you *actually chose*.

## Final Word

### *(and It's an Important One)*

This whole book hasn't really been about decisions. It's been about **you**.

The version of you that's more powerful than they were told. The version of you that's finally stopped waiting. The version of you that knows it was never about being sure, it was about being **courageous**.

So go on.

Start the business. Make the call. Quit the job. Double your prices. Tell them how you feel. Launch the damn thing.

Not recklessly. Not stupidly. Just finally.

***Because ... Training yourself to say "F*** It" first, fear loses its grip and courage takes over.***

# Acknowledgments

To my family who asked, “How’s the book going?” thank you. That question kept me focused and helped. To every reader who picks this book up and whispers, “F*** It”, I’m ready...” I wrote this for you.

Now go decide on something that scares you, have a red-hot go because life is short and **risk is better than regret.**

# Reader's Challenge: Make One Big Decision This Week

You've made it to the end of this book. That means something inside you is ready.

**Now, it's your move:** Make one bold decision this week that you've been putting off—big or small, it just needs to scare you a little and move you forward a lot.

- Set a timer: 24 hours.
- Make the call.
- Send the email.
- Have the conversation.

Just move. If you whisper "F*** It" right before you act, perfect. You're doing it right.

# Recommended Resources: Books, Podcasts and YouTube

## BOOKS:

- ✓ **The Hour Between Dog and Wolf** – Author: John Coates
- ✓ **Courage is Calling** – Author: Ryan Holiday
- ✓ **The Motivation Manifesto** – Author: Brendon Burchard
- ✓ **The Power of Regret** – Author: Daniel H Pink
- ✓ **Start with Why** - Author: Simon Sinek
- ✓ **Purpose Meaning and Passion** – Author: Harvard Business Review
- ✓ **The Greatest Salesman in the World** – Author: Og Mandino
- ✓ **Four Thousand Weeks** – Author: Oliver Burkeman
- ✓ **Daring Greatly** – Author: Brene' Brown
- ✓ **The Wim Hoff Method** – Author: Wim Hoff
- ✓ **The Art of Resilience** – Author: Ross Edgley

## PODCASTS:

- ✓ **The Daily Stoic** – Host: Ryan Holiday
- ✓ **The School of Greatness** – Host: Lewis Hamilton
- ✓ **The Diary of A CEO** – Host: Steven Bartlett
- ✓ **The Knowledge Project** – Host: Shane Parrish
- ✓ **A Bit of Optimism** – Host: Simon Sinek
- ✓ **Huberman Lab** – Host: Andrew Huberman
- ✓ **Straight Talk with Mark Bouris** – Host: Mark Bouris

## YOUTUBE:

- ✓ The Time You Have (In Jellybeans)
- ✓ the power of CHOICE (a short film)
- ✓ If by Rudyard Kipling - Read by Sir Michael Caine
- ✓ Nothing changes if nothing changes.

# About the Author

Andre Elcham is an entrepreneur who's built several startups, including Deus Nexus, helping businesses cut through the noise and get things done.

He's made a career out of saying "F*** It" and figuring it out, whether launching a retail brand with limited fashion experience or growing an HR firm from scratch.

Today, he works with founders and executives to bring clarity to chaos and momentum to indecision. He runs on coffee and still believes: **Risk Is Better Than Regret.**